PRESTON
THEN & NOW
IN COLOUR

JOHN GARLINGTON

The History Press

To Nina, Ruth & Beth

First published in 2012, this edition 2015

The History Press
The Mill, Brimscombe Port
Stroud, Gloucestershire, GL5 2QG
www.thehistorypress.co.uk

British Library Cataloguing in Publication Data.
A catalogue record for this book is available from the British Library.

ISBN 978 0 7509 6372 5

Typesetting and origination by The History Press
Printed in China.

CONTENTS

ACKNOWLEDGEMENTS

The majority of the older images are reproduced from my family's collection. For the rest I would like to thank the Harris Museum and Art Gallery for their kind permission to reproduce photographs of the Obelisk, Winckley Square, in 1855, and the six by Robert Pateson depicting Avenham, Winckley Square, Fishergate and Cheapside.

I would like to thank the acting Principal of Cardinal Newman College for allowing me access to the building and grounds at Lark Hill to take four photographs there, and Claire Johnson for making arrangements.

As always, I would like to thank my wife, Nina, and my daughters, Ruth and Beth, for their encouragement, help and advice.

ABOUT THE AUTHOR

Fascinated by the history of Preston, his home city, John Garlington has written several books on the subject and has an extensive collection of old postcards of the area. He is also the biographer of Robert Pateson, the Preston photographer and scientist; wrote a history of Preston's war memorial, designed by Sir Giles Gilbert Scott; has researched and documented the seven Catholic First World War memorials in Preston; and has written an outline history of the city's St Walburge's church.

INTRODUCTION

There is a temptation, when looking at old photographs, to think that the lives of the people caught in them are mainly similar, or even partly similar, to the lives we lead now. The old pictures in this book were mostly taken about a hundred years ago and show a city (or town, as it was then) which retained its medieval town plan, but had completely removed any evidence of its medieval past. The buildings in the older images were mostly developed after 1840 when wealth, accumulated during the Industrial Revolution, especially in a period of peace and prosperity from 1855-75, was put to civic, philanthropic and economic purposes. The well-to-do lived on the fringes of the Victorian town, in new suburbs such as Fulwood and Ashton, or even as near as St Thomas's Road, being a carriage ride away from town. Others, such as lawyers, doctors and other professionals, lived in the area of Avenham east of Frenchwood Street, through Ribblesdale Place and into the streets around Winckley Square. There was, in streets clustered on the edge of Avenham, a small colony of artists and musicians. Another such community lived behind Bow Lane and Fishergate Hill.

The 1911 census shows that the population of Preston was just under 120,000 and the distribution of wealth within it more than likely reflected the national statistic that the richest 1 per cent of the population in 1911-13 owned 69 per cent of the wealth. As a result, many families in the town lived in low-quality terraced houses, mostly grouped around cotton mills and factories. Most of these were small, the more modern of which had a toilet in its back yard. Some may have had access to hot water. There were many more children. In 1914, every third person in the United Kingdom was a child under the age of fourteen. The modern equivalent is one in fifteen. The majority of Prestonians were working class, a fact supported by the rough statistic that only 0.7 per cent of the men killed from the town in the First World War were officers. Official British Army sources show that 4 per cent of the whole force killed were officers.

In contrast, perhaps not as great as some may have imagined, 20 per cent of the population of the United Kingdom own 62 per cent of the wealth at the time of writing. The present poor financial situation has encouraged some experts to predict that a return to Edwardian, even Victorian, conditions is a possibility. Before I began taking the present-day photographs, I had the impression that the city was in a state of change, a feeling that other Prestonians might share. My mind was quickly changed as I made my tour. I realised that the time of change has gone, for the time being, and at the present the city is in a state of stagnation. Some areas that were once vibrant commercial centres are now bordering on lifeless. The centre is dominated by the car and filled with national chain stores. Some older buildings do stand preserved, though others have unfortunately been demolished or stand empty. In some cases buildings have been and gone in the century in between, showing the comparatively transient quality of modern designs in comparison to those of the Victorian and Edwardian periods.

Except in two instances, the images I chose to partner the older photographs have certain common reference points, which should help the reader to make their own judgements.

FISHERGATE
LOOKING WEST

FISHERGATE IN ABOUT 1950. With one or two exceptions, Fishergate still retains its Edwardian appearance, even down to the road surface of setts. On the extreme right are the unexpanded *Lancashire Evening Post* premises. Further down looms the spirelet of the church-like Gas Board offices. In the distance are the cupola of the Shelley building and the clock tower of the Fishergate Baptist Church.

WITH THE EXCEPTION of two buildings, almost everything in the 1950s picture has changed. On the extreme right, the *Lancashire Evening Post* offices and print rooms were demolished when the newspaper moved to purpose-built premises in Fulwood. In the distance, the green dome of the former Shelley building on the corner of Lune Street is visible, though the Gas Board offices were demolished in 1964 to make way for St George's Shopping Centre. The only other survivor is the Marks & Spencer building, still on the site where the company first opened a shop in 1905.

FRIARGATE
LOOKING SOUTH

FRIARGATE LOOKING SOUTH, from Heatley Street corner, probably in around 1946. This unusual view illustrates admirably how the Scott's Town Hall dominated Preston from 1867 to 1947 and how its clock was clearly visible by day and night when it was illuminated. Victorian shopkeepers used to send their shop boys into the street to check the time. Further down on the right, the gable-ended frontage belongs to the Old Black Bull that now stands on the corner by the modern ring road, which cuts right across Friargate.

THIS VIEW FROM Friargate Brow was never popular with postcard photographers, yet it shows a way into the town centre through one of its three medieval thoroughfares. In the distance is the refashioned Crystal House, which took the place of the fire damaged Town Hall. Further forward on the right are the recently built shops of St George's Shopping Centre. The gable-ended frontage of the Old Black Bull is still just visible, though it now stands on the corner of Ringway, the ring road which was cut through the town in the early 1970s.

THE OBELISK
AND FISH
STONES

THE OBELISK AND Fish Stones, Flag Market, about 1853.
The obelisk – really a clustered column – was the second to
stand here and the last of many similar fitments, such as
market crosses, on this square before being removed and
made into gateposts at Hollowforth Hall in 1853. Built
in 1782 after the collapse of the original, the obelisk was
installed with a gas lamp in 1816, thus illuminating Preston's
market in a unique way for the time. The fish stones, placed
nearby in 1605, were also cleared away in 1853. The square
was flagged in 1867.

THE ONLY REMAINING building from the 1853 photograph,
now attributed to Silas Eastham, is the small gable-ended
shop on the left. It is thought to be oldest building in the town.

In the centre is the straightened and widened southern end of Friargate and the red-brick building to the right is on the corner of Market Street, which was created in 1893, sweeping away most of the shops, eating houses and warehouses on the Eastham's image. This new street was built straight and wide, in complete contrast to the side streets, alleys and courts it replaced.

WINCKLEY SQUARE – NORTH-EAST CORNER

NORTH-EAST CORNER of Winckley Square,
*c.*1853. Until 1801, most of this area was a large
open space known as Town End Field, which was
bought by Thomas Winckley. He developed it into
a square, kept apart from the rest of the town
centre, which became a prestigious place to live
in or near. The houses had mostly Georgian-style
frontages with neo-classical doorways and
patterned railings. To the left are the gardens
which were held privately by the house owners,
who each had a key to their plot. The original
photograph is a small ambrotype

THERE ARE SOME remnants of the older image here, but peace and quiet are not two of them. Thomas Winckley's idea of land kept apart from the town centre has given way to a noisy, busy thoroughfare edged with double yellow lines. In the distance is Thomas Miller's house, now divided up into apartments after eighty years as a school. Most of the original buildings remain, but a parking meter has taken the place of the servant in the doorway on the right. The railings were never replaced after their wartime removal.

AVENHAM LANE

AVENHAM LANE, 1862, photographed by Robert Pateson. One of the town's oldest thoroughfares, Avenham Lane was, and still is, a road of contrasts. In front of the camera, which is looking west, is a charming and prosperous scene. The bow-fronted house was owned by George Sharples, a successful pharmacist of the time. In the distance are the gates of Avenham Walk and to the right is the portico of Avenham House, demolished in 1890 to make

way for a road-widening scheme.
Behind the camera was an area
inhabited by the families of cotton
workers, artisans, and labourers,
which worsened the further east a
person travelled.

ONCE A PEACEFUL lane in every
sense of the word, this road
is now a through route from
Avenham Park to London Road.
Pateson chose this as an artistic,
topographical photograph whose
human interest was the young
Burton brothers. The man is
possibly their father, John Burton,
who was Pateson's early patron
and is standing outside his front
door. In the distance is the corner
of Avenham Colonnade and the
car coming towards the camera
creates a good contrast to the horse
and carriage in the older image.

WINCKLEY SQUARE –
SOUTH-WEST CORNER

THE SOUTH-WEST corner of Winckley Square, 1862, by Robert Pateson. These fine residences on the west side of the square are all basically in the Georgian style, which has made it famous

among students of architecture. No. 23, with the projecting portico, was the home of Thomas Batty Addison, thought by some to be Charles Dickens' model for Josiah Bounderby in *Hard Times*. In the foreground are the gates which were closed at night and a small gate leading to a private garden. The railings were removed in 1940, but fortunately replaced fifty years later. One can just about make out a boy on the steps of No. 22.

THIS PAIRING IS another in this book which completely misses a well-known institution, in this case Winckley Square Convent School, which occupied these houses from 1875 to 1981. At the moment the premises are mostly divided into apartments but there is a restaurant in No. 23, Addison's former residence. The corner of the garden was used by the school as a sports field until fields down at Riverside were bought in 1910. The holly tree, in the centre of Pateson's image, continues to flourish today.

CORNER OF CROSS STREET AND WINCKLEY SQUARE

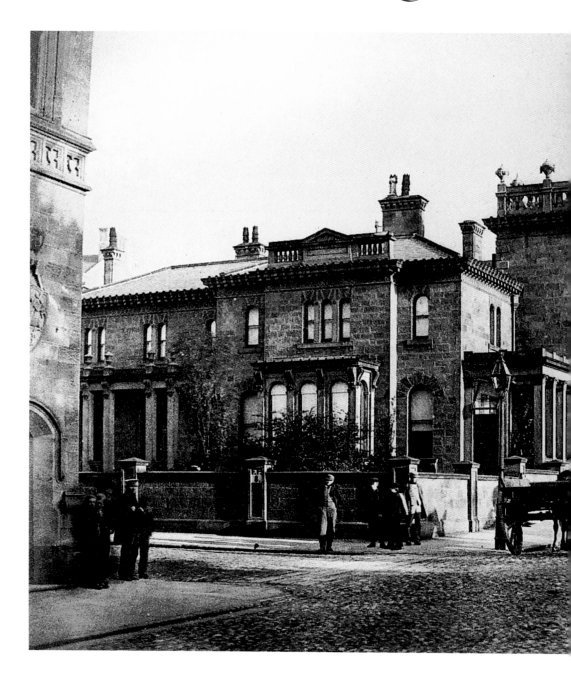

CORNER OF CROSS Street and Winckley Square, 1862, by Robert Pateson. This magnificent view shows Thomas Ainsworth's villa, built in an Italian style in 1850, thus completing the square and complementing the good architectural style already there. Ainsworth was a wealthy cotton magnate with a factory off Church Street, where working conditions were very harsh. In the 1940s the villa became a county court office and was eventually demolished in 1969. Its successor is a dreadful red-brick office block.

ALTHOUGH IT MAY be too much to expect that streets and buildings in a busy town will be in the same state as they were 150 years ago, it might be expected in a town square where the Georgian frontages of the houses were regarded as remarkable as any in England, that the general view of the original planners and developers would be respected and preserved. This eastern side of the square, as far as style is concerned, has been completely wrecked, especially by this red-brick office block.

19

WINCKLEY SQUARE
FROM THE SOUTH-EAST

WINCKLEY SQUARE FROM the south-east, 1862, by Robert Pateson. Looking down this side of the square, the tower of Ainsworth's villa, the minarets of the Winckley Club and, on the left, gates to the private south side can be seen. Some houses, almost all now used as offices, have been fairly carefully preserved, as has the one on the left, but some have been rebuilt without much thought, especially on this side. Serious proposals to make the square a car park in 1970 were quashed, but traffic makes it a busy place during the day. Described in 1880 as having 'emerald charm and propriety of culture', Winckley Square still seems like a retreat from the town centre rush.

IN 1969, AINSWORTH'S villa was surrounded by high screens and was systematically demolished. After that, for some weeks, anyone who lived, worked or was educated on the square was subjected to the incessant pounding of piles being driven into the ground for the foundations of the red office block to the right. The poet, John Betjeman, always a guardian of good taste, would probably have described the building as barbaric in appearance. Although the minarets of the Winckley Club have gone, the trees in the garden have achieved a beauty planned by the original developers.

FISHERGATE NEAR THE BAPTIST CHURCH

GUILD ARCH, FISHERGATE, in 1862, by Robert Pateson. Ghostly figures on both sides give an idea of the long exposure needed to take this photograph. Every twenty years Preston celebrates

the Guild Merchant and temporary decorated arches welcome visitors. To the left is the newly built Fishergate Baptist Church and opposite is the Theatre Royal. Just further on, the one-storey shop is one of the oldest in the town. The bill posters advertise the Guild Ball and an opera at the Theatre Royal. All this right side is now occupied by the Fishergate Centre.

THIS IMAGE CLEARLY shows the effect of change in the centre of the city. The only constant is Fishergate Baptist Church on the left. The buildings to the right, known as the Fishergate Centre, stand on the site of the ABC cinema, which succeeded the Theatre Royal, just visible in Pateson's photograph. One of the oldest shops in Preston, just visible in the 1862 image, was demolished to make way for a Marks & Spencer store. When they rebuilt, a suggestion of its classical frontage was put into the new design. Robert Pateson is possibly the man with his back to the camera in the older image.

23

SITE OF THE TOWN HALL, CHEAPSIDE

THE OLD TOWN Hall, photographed in 1862 by Robert Pateson. This site, now occupied by Crystal House, is in the process of being cleared. In the first phase, ancient houses occupied during Guild Week celebrations were demolished. The second phase held a similar fate for the rest, including the old Town Hall (left), completed in 1782, but too small by 1862 for council business. One clock face survived, the clock being sold to a farmer near Kirkham, and the cupola, built to house it in 1814, was relocated on the Public Hall. The new Town Hall's foundation stone was laid during the 1862 Guild Week celebrations.

WHEN PATESON TOOK his photograph in 1862, the town was about to celebrate the 1862 Guild and the city is now about to celebrate the Guild of 2012. He could hardly have imagined that the 'new' Town Hall, designed by George Gilbert Scott, would only survive as a working building for eighty years and a second, Crystal House, would take its place. This view, taken from exactly the same angle on Cheapside, shows the south-west corner of the recently remodelled Crystal House, with the white façade of Waterstone's in the distance.

FISHERGATE NEAR THE RAILWAY STATION

SHOPS IN FISHERGATE near the railway station, probably 1897. These premises were built in around 1845. No. 53, left, is the Alexandra Hotel, which had recently been taken over by Hannah Richardson, the next-door neighbour, in 1894. William Tuson, a draper who also sold floor coverings,

owned No. 54, from where trading continued under his name until 1943. Should anyone be in doubt, the Railway Drug Store was owned by John Jackson, whose window is cluttered with stock. Judging by the royal crests, Queen Victoria's Diamond Jubilee was being celebrated.

THIS IMAGE SHOWS one of the starkest changes in the collection: the shop windows for Fishergate Centre units, the main feature here being those of Debenhams. It also represents the general shift of shopping from smaller businesses to large, nationwide concerns. As a result, shops which once stood here on the way to the railway station, including an optician's, a number of small restaurants and an antiques business, gave way in 1984 to a building which some have appropriately described as 'railway vernacular'. The necessary traffic lights and bollards are very much in evidence here.

FISHERGATE BY VICTORIA BUILDINGS

VICTORIA BUILDINGS IN about 1932. This view shows the growing influence of the car, as Wade's Bazaar has given way to Loxham's Garage, surmounted by the legend 'The Age of the Motor Car'. Further on is the imposing Fishergate Baptist Church, designed by James Hibbert and

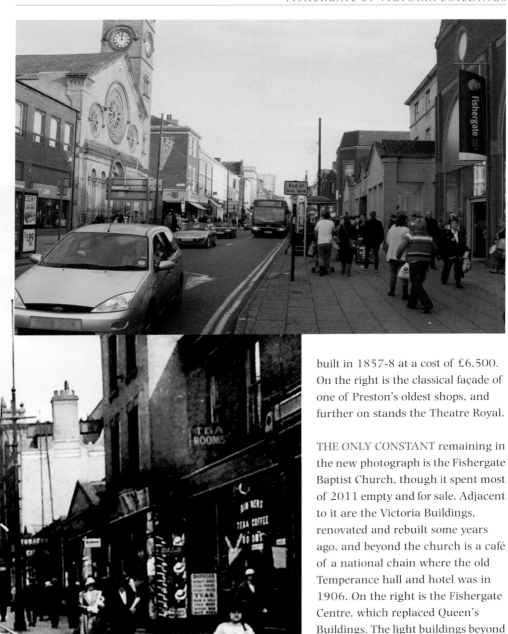

built in 1857-8 at a cost of £6,500. On the right is the classical façade of one of Preston's oldest shops, and further on stands the Theatre Royal.

THE ONLY CONSTANT remaining in the new photograph is the Fishergate Baptist Church, though it spent most of 2011 empty and for sale. Adjacent to it are the Victoria Buildings, renovated and rebuilt some years ago, and beyond the church is a café of a national chain where the old Temperance hall and hotel was in 1906. On the right is the Fishergate Centre, which replaced Queen's Buildings. The light buildings beyond reflect the ancient, classically fronted shop just visible in the old image, once the premises of Thornton and France, wine merchants, which was demolished in 1985.

FISHERGATE NEAR FOX STREET

FISHERGATE NEAR FOX Street, *c.*1906. The delicate tinting of this postcard ensured that no fine detail was lost. On the left, up to the ivy-covered building on Fox Street corner, are the shops owned by Brocklehurst and Sons, tailors; John Frame, tourist director, and James Jamieson, the photographer, worked at these premises from 1904-1932. Richard Brocklehurst was successful

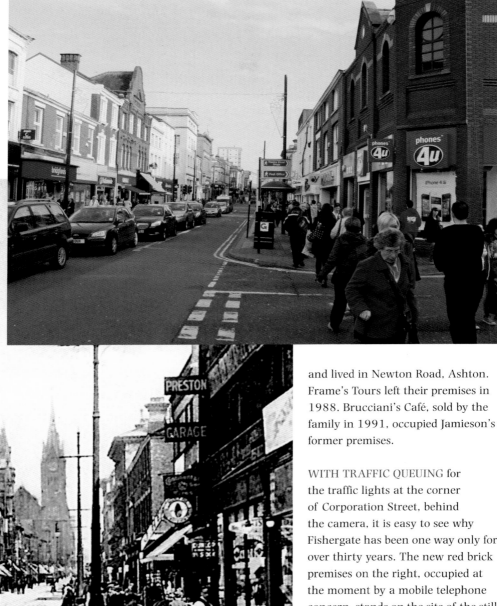

and lived in Newton Road, Ashton. Frame's Tours left their premises in 1988. Brucciani's Café, sold by the family in 1991, occupied Jamieson's former premises.

WITH TRAFFIC QUEUING for the traffic lights at the corner of Corporation Street, behind the camera, it is easy to see why Fishergate has been one way only for over thirty years. The new red brick premises on the right, occupied at the moment by a mobile telephone concern, stands on the site of the still much missed Theatre Hotel. On the left, surrounded by a building society, estate agents', bakery shop and a fast-food store, stands the only shop which retains its original frontage – Brucciani's Café.

FISHERGATE, CORNER OF BIRLEY STREET

TOWN HALL, FISHERGATE, *c.*1907. Forty years of pollution have darkened the Longridge stone from its original state. The clock used Westminster chimes, which at times could be heard from great distances away; some people used to forecast the weather from the sound of the clock chimes. Based on the medieval Cloth Hall at Ypres, officials from there came to see the Town Hall before rebuilding the war-shattered Cloth Hall in 1919. Partly destroyed by fire on 15 March 1947, the Town Hall remnant was cleared in 1962. Its whitewood dance floor was sold for firewood and the stone was ground down and used as reinforcement in the sea banking at Clifton.

THE SUCCESSOR TO the Town Hall's truncated remains after the fire in 1947 was Crystal House, which was hated by many when it was completed in 1962. There had been appeals for the open space to be kept as a piazza. By 2008 the twelve-storey office block was showing signs of wear and tear. Much of it was discoloured, many of the pebble-dash facings were cracked and office windows had yellowed sheets of paper covering them to keep the sun out. It is no wonder that Prestonians voted it overwhelmingly as the building they most wanted to see demolished. Work started on its refurbishment later that year.

FRIARGATE NEAR ORCHARD STREET

FRIARGATE NEAR ORCHARD Street, c.1925. This is another of Preston's ancient thoroughfares, taking its name from the small pre-Reformation priory sited nearby. On the right is Tyler's bootmakers and next door is Slinger and Sons, who seemed to make and sell every sort of tool imaginable for home and work. Just beyond is the steel and glass portico of the Royal Hippodrome Theatre. Built in 1896, this theatre presented variety, music hall and drama. In 1947 the Salberg Players began their

repertory, putting on 365 plays, until March 1955. All these buildings were pulled down to make way for C&A in 1959.

RATHER THAN BEING completely pedestrianised, many streets in the city, like the upper part of Friargate, are traffic restricted. To the left is the entrance to St George's Shopping Centre, which was once the way into a collection of old streets, full of shops, known as Bamber's Yard, as shown in the older image. On the right is the Black Horse public house, where a survivor of the Charge of the Light Brigade worked as a stable hand in his later years. Further on is the glass-fronted premises occupied, until 2000, by C&A.

LOWER FRIARGATE LOOKING NORTH

LOWER FRIARGATE, *c.*1906. Largely ignored by photographers in general, this gives a rare view of lower Friargate. Off this road ran many small alleys and streets formed in the early nineteenth century, the base for the Catholic community round St Mary's (demolished in 1993). Hill Street, Hope Street, Edward Street and Heatley Street are survivors of this period. In the distance is Adelphi Street, and the Adelphi Hotel (established in 1774) stands on Fylde Street. Behind this stands Henry Shutt's corn mill (pulled down in 1994),

one of the last reminders of the period up to 1830 when agriculture and windmills began and Friargate finished.

THE ADELPHI HOTEL still stands on the corner of Adelphi Street and Kendal Street, or Canal Street as it was known until 1932. Most people would not even know of its existence today as it only consists of two large, busy roundabouts. Behind the Adelphi is a landscaped space where Shutt's Corn Mill once stood and beyond that can just be seen the university buildings clustered round St Peter's Square. The white building on the left is the empty premises of Bamber's Furnishers, a firm which ceased trading in 2011 after over 100 years.

THE FLAG MARKET
LOOKING NORTH

THE FLAG MARKET looking north, 1903. This view of the Flag Market is very unusual. The modern view from this spot is obscured by the Obelisk (replaced in 1977) and the trees , which were planted in 1925. Now the area is cluttered with traffic signs and yellow lines. A year later the stanchions for tram power lines were erected and the Boer War memorial built in front of the post office. The small building on the left is one of Preston's oldest buildings, built in around 1640. The shadow in the foreground is cast by one of the Town Hall's pinnacles.

THE FLAG MARKET was one of the ancient market places of the city until the 1970s when all the stalls which appeared on four days were moved to the new indoor market hall on

Liverpool Street. The black shape in the middle is the crib, which is put out during Advent each year. On the right is the war memorial, designed by Sir Giles Gilbert Scott, which was unveiled by Lord Jellicoe in 1926. Behind it is the former general post office, which now lies mostly empty. To the right of the crib is a tree which managed to survive a council cull.

CHEAPSIDE FROM FRIARGATE CORNER

TOWN HALL AND Cheapside, by Arthur Shaw of Blackburn, *c*.1910. Dominating this is the
north side of the Town Hall, opened on 2 October 1867. Its 198ft tower was raised one storey
from the original plan so that its clock could be seen from the station. When illuminated,
the clock could be seen in parts of the Fylde and from ships in the Ribble Estuary. It had five

TOWN HALL & MARKET PLACE, PRESTON.

bells using Westminster chimes. The largest, weighing four and a half tons, was the most powerful in Britain after Big Ben and St Paul's. The chimes went wrong in the 1890s, forcing the council to act when it struck twenty-two during a morning council meeting.

THIS ROAD IS one of the oldest in the city and bears a medieval name. It was called Cheapside because it ran by one of the markets, or 'cheaps' as they were known in the Middle Ages. Recently, some of the trees planted in 1925 were removed as their foliage had become too luxuriant and had begun to obscure the general view in summer. It is thought that some of them had been planted originally beside the South African war memorial and were moved when it was replaced by the present memorial.

THE FLAG MARKET
LOOKING SOUTH

THE FLAG MARKET, 1952. On 15 March 1947, after a police function, a fire broke out in the
ballroom and quickly spread. The magnificent tower was literally its own downfall, acting like a
burning chimney, drawing in air from the street. At 3.45 a.m. the clock chimed for the last time
as fire engulfed the mechanism – at which moment the spire crashed into Fishergate. Then a

great death knell sounded as falling timbers and masonry struck the bells which fell loudly, and finally, down the tower. A truncated version continued in some use until 1962. Crystal House now occupies the site.

AFTER THE FRONT of the Town Hall was destroyed, the remaining building became largely neglected and pigeons took residence under the arches on Fishergate. Because Scott had drawn on the design of the Cloth Hall at Ypres, badly damaged by shellfire during 1916-18, representatives came to Preston to look at the Town Hall after the Great War. When the Town Hall was damaged no one from Preston Council went to Ypres to see the rebuilt Cloth Hall. These days, the Flag Market is the venue for events such as European Markets or concerts.

LANCASTER ROAD

LANCASTER ROAD, *c.*1910. On the left is the Miller Arcade; on the right is Starkie's Corner, so called because of Starkie's gentleman's outfitters. Past the arcade is the east frontage and entrance to the Harris Library, and further on is the Sessions House, completed in 1903. An open space after that is the Cinder Pad where the Municipal Offices were opened in 1933. Beyond this is the balustraded tower of the police station. In the foreground on the right are two of the controversial ornamental tram cable poles.

THIS SOUTHERN END of Lancaster Road was, until the 1890s, a row of butchers' premises and shops where goods were displayed openly and slaughtering took place. The Victorian buildings on the right, with quasi-classical frontages, were built in 1854 and are listed buildings. Just beyond the bus and the trees can be glimpsed the jutting frontage of the Guild Hall, which was built for the Guild of 1972, though it was completed too late because the foundations had been put in the wrong place. At the end of the Arcade is the ornamental doorway which led to the Turkish Baths.

LANCASTER ROAD FROM CHURCH STREET

LANCASTER ROAD CORNER from Church Street, c.1908. Starkie's, the outfitters on the corner, boasted that their goods were sold 'at the smallest possible profit', adding quickly 'for ready money only'. Next door is Birchall's tobacconists and next to them are the premises of Breakell and Co., a very successful wine merchant and proprietors of 'Real Stingo Whiskey'. They brewed beer, bottled Guinness, provided brewing materials for pubs and had a bonded warehouse in Avenham Street. The gateway on the right leads to the stables of the old coaching

inn, The Red Lion, now aptly renamed The Coach House.

THE MILLER ARCADE has turned out to be a survivor, despite the loss of its 'pepper pot' towers in the 1930s for safety reasons. The window nearest to the camera belonged to The King's Arms and Hayworth's Wine Stores, Lancaster Road. During the last twenty years it was occupied by a school outfitters and a sports shop, but now it is occupied by a business which is a café during the day and a club at night. The toilets in the centre of Church Street have been removed but their wrought-iron railings have been preserved on the pavement nearby.

THE MILLER ARCADE

THE MILLER ARCADE, 1902. The arcade covers an area originally occupied by a dozen or more premises, including part of the Old Shambles in Lancaster Road. Designed by Edwin Bush, it was opened in 1898. Covered by a terracotta façade, the structure is basically a steel frame. After being

a centre of activity, its custom and appearance suffered in the 1960s. Known as Arndale House after its acquisition in 1958, Miller Arcade's condition caused an outcry and demolition came close in 1970. It was rescued, refurbished and had its name restored, and happily it prospers today.

THE MILLER ARCADE was based on the design for Burlington Arcade in London, which was the first purpose-built arcade of its type. The firm that built it to Edwin Bush's design went to New York shortly after to build skyscrapers. The arrangement of offices on the first floor and shops on the ground has mostly worked well. Both the Football League and Preston North End were once administered from here. The introduction of doors at each point of entry keeps the interior free of the pigeons and rubbish which once plagued it.

CHURCH STREET NEAR GRIMSHAW STREET

CHURCH STREET, NEAR Grimshaw Street, *c*.1910. Church Street was a thriving shopping area until 1960, when commercial emphasis shifted to Fishergate, especially after St George's Shopping Centre was opened in 1965. In Church Street in 1910 all manner of goods could be bought, including: stationery; shoes; food, both cooked and

fresh; drinks, alcoholic or not; anything for babies and children; smokers' requisites; medicines, herbal or otherwise; books; newspapers; musical instruments; tripe; brushes; photographs; plants; and seeds.

NO OTHER PHOTOGRAPH in this collection shows deterioration and decline like this one. No other pairing shows such a marked difference as this. A glance at the modern view may give the reader the impression that there is little difference, but there are only a handful of shops still trading. However, the shop on the corner on the right is a nationally known record shop. There are no bus stops in this street anymore, and premises are boarded up. One which is not boarded up can be seen on the extreme right and may be the most corroded shop in the city.

THE PRISON FROM CHURCH STREET

THE PRISON FROM Church Street, *c.*1906. Heavy traffic thunders past this point now, making the Edwardian image very rural in comparison. Notice the street sweeper in the road. The prison, built in 1789, was visited by Elizabeth Fry and John Gurney, and was found to be one of the best. In 1911 an otherwise good report revealed that there had been some cell wrecking, recommending

that the best punishment would be the birch or the cat-o'-nine-tails. Closed in 1930, it was re-opened after the war and today houses about 600 inmates.

ALTHOUGH THE MAIN characteristics of the older image are still in evidence, the modern traffic situation on this, the A6, had the author skipping from traffic island to traffic island, trying to achieve a similar angle. On the right, the old militia barracks now contain the Lancashire Museum which has very recently been refurbished. In the centre is the crenellated frontage of the main building and to the left is the main gatehouse. The A6 runs into the city along London Road, into Stanley Street (right) then into Ringway, which now occupies what was Park Road.

ST IGNATIUS'S WAR MEMORIAL

ST IGNATIUS'S WAR memorial unveiling, 26 March 1922. By 1917 the parish had decided a memorial was needed as 120 men had been killed (rising to 228 in 1918). A penny fund was started and £150 was raised for an outdoor memorial with all the names inscribed. In the presence of a huge crowd it was unveiled by Colonel John Shute CMG, DSO, and a year later a memorial window was put in the Lady Chapel. The house on the extreme right, No. 12, was once occupied by Francis Thompson's parents. Note the dark colour of the once white church extensions built in 1912.

THE CHURCH WAS cleaned of all its industrial staining for the 1972 Guild and now looks much as it would have in the 1830s. The parish, originally staffed by priests of the Society of Jesus, was left in the hands of Catholic clergy in 1958. The memorial has aged well in one area but not in others. The plaques show as clearly as they may have done in 1921. Unfortunately, ninety years of wind and rain have weathered the whole structure quite badly. The faces of the crucified Christ and the servicemen have corroded into skeletal sharpness and the rifles have almost worn away.

GARSTANG ROAD LOOKING SOUTH

GARSTANG ROAD LOOKING south, *c.*1914. In the distance can be seen the crossroads with Addison (Blackpool) Road and the trees on the left mark the corner of Victoria Road. In the early part of the last century this road was improved between Preston and Lancaster. The section between Moor Lane and the Withy Trees was widened in 1817, getting rid of all the hillocks and depressions which made travelling so tedious and dangerous.

THIS IS THE A6, one of the busiest roads in the area. In the distance is the junction with Blackpool Road. It is one of the most dangerous crossings in the city. In the Victorian and Edwardian periods this was a quiet and select area for the well-to-do, being a longer carriage ride from the town centre. For a hundred years, until the 1990s, this was a self-contained shopping area for the community. Within walking distance there was a butcher's, a confectioner's, three newsagents', a chemist's, a dentist's, a doctor's, a post office, a general store and a garage.

WITHY TREES CROSSROADS, FULWOOD

WITHY TREES CROSSROADS, Fulwood, *c*.1925. Taken from the garden of Fulwood Methodist Church, this view shows Garstang Road, from left to right crossing, with Watling Street Road running over to Lytham Road (called Watling Street Road West until 1912). On the left is Withy Trees garage, demolished in the 1970s to be replaced with a more gaudy arrangement. To its left are two houses called Withy Grove, built in 1879, and in the centre is the Withy Trees Hotel, built in the early nineteenth century.

THOUGHT TO BE one of the more dangerous junctions in the city, this crossroads did not have traffic lights until fifty years ago. In the centre is Withy Grove, once two houses with gardens, now occupied by a mobility business and a chemist, whose extravagant hoarding covers the plaque 'Withy Grove 1879'. There has been an inn on the site of the 200-year-old Withy Trees for three centuries. When the development known as Fulwood Park was started nearby, the sale of alcohol was forbidden, so the Withy Trees became very popular. Its famous bowling green is now a beer garden.

BLACK BULL LANE, FULWOOD

BLACK BULL LANE, *c*.1930. Until 1820, Black Bull Lane – or Cadley Road, as it was then called – was the main route to Lancaster. The main road turned left after the Withy Trees toll bar before turning right into the valley of Savick Brook in Cadley Road. In winter the road was often impassable as horse-pulling heavy vehicles, especially important stagecoaches, could not grip the surface on the inclines, causing many delays. The problem was solved by

constructing the Withy Trees and Sharoe Green section of Garstang Road.

IMAGES OF PRESTON in 2011 show a few premises being repaired or extended like this Spar shop, which has had a long history going back 100 years as a general store and bakery, being owned by both the Garth and Towers families in turn. Looking past the roundabout in the centre, the semi-rural nature of the area has gone in favour of pre-war housing. On the extreme right is the extension to the Derby School, which was built after the war and now serves as a home for people with special needs.

DERBY SCHOOL/LODGE, FULWOOD

THE HOME FOR the Blind, 1900, by Edwin Beattie. A scheme for blind employment was financed in 1864 by Joseph Livesey, the famous Preston abstainer. It was such a success that a number of premises were outgrown before the home was opened in 1895. Dormitories were built and resident scholars were taken in. Blind and partially sighted children were evacuated here from Liverpool in 1939, but only the blind returned in 1945, when the school specialised, successfully, with partially sighted pupils. Despite parental resistance, the school was sold and converted into offices.

NOW KNOWN AS Derby Lodge, the appearance of the building has changed very little since Edwin Beattie created his drawing of it for Anthony Hewitson's *Northward* book in 1900. Just before education for partially sighted children was provided elsewhere, the words 'Home for the Blind' were erased from the large stone plaque. The premises are occupied now by solicitors, accountants and a women only gym. Ironically, and perhaps appropriately, children still have a tenuous link with the building: the area office of Barnardo's is here.

TULKETH MILL

TULKETH MILL CHIMNEY
maintenance, 1925. The
factory was the spinning half
of a twin scheme with weaving,
which was never built, though
extensions were made in 1918.
At its peak in 1930 the mill
worked 126,864 mule spindles
and 12,000 ring spindles to
spin American and Egyptian
(sakel) yarn. Its lodges both
held 1,750,000 gallons of
water, and the machinery
was powered by a 2,000hp
horizontal cross-component
engine. The building is now
used by the Peter Craig
mail-order firm.

THIS MAGNIFICENT EDWARDIAN structure, built with such high hopes, still stands mostly intact. After the mail-order firm left, the site was leased by the Carphone Warehouse, its present occupiers. For about eighteen months after the demolition of factories and warehouses, the building stood in full, splendid view of Blackpool Road, as it did in the older image. The road itself was constructed in 1922 when the Serpentine, Addison Road and Long Lane in Ashton were joined together and bridges were built over railways and the canal to create a route to Blackpool away from the town centre.

THE GRAMMAR SCHOOL, CROSS STREET

PRESTON GRAMMAR SCHOOL, Cross Street, *c.*1905. Effectively begun in 1468, the school was run in premises near the parish church until 1841 when new buildings, designed in the perpendicular style, with Moorish domes by John Welch, were opened. Thomas Duckett carved the decorations including the school badge, the portcullis. The whole building and contents were bought in 1860 by the Corporation for £1,500. On the left are Sir Robert Peel's statue and the Winckley Club and Philosophical Society buildings.

THE GRAMMAR SCHOOL buildings look fine, but when a thorough examination of the town was made by *The Builder* magazine in 1861, it was found that the school did not provide toilets for the pupils. The boys had to go in the corners of the playground. The buildings on the right were demolished in early 1960s to make way for this utilitarian office block, once occupied by Lancashire County Council but now empty and up for sale. The statue of Robert Peel was the focus of a tribute in 1928 by the Catholic community for his involvement in Catholic Emancipation in 1832.

ST VINCENT'S ORPHANAGE

ST VINCENT'S CATHOLIC Poor Law School, St Vincent's Road, 1900, drawn by Edwin Beattie. This large turreted red-brick establishment was opened on the east side of Garstang Road in 1896 with room for 300 boys. A sum of £6,000 was needed for the project and a Grand Bazaar at the Public Hall raised £7,179 in November 1891. Run by the Sisters of St Vincent de Paul, St Vincent's performed a great social and educational service for deprived boys until it was closed in 1961. A small remaining part of the school is still used by Corpus Christi Roman Catholic High School.

IN HIS DRAWING, taken from Anthony Hewitson's *Northward* book, Beattie has depicted more than St Vincent's School, which was demolished in 1961. To the left are some of the buildings of the Jeanne Jugan Residence, known to Preston Catholics as the Little Sisters of the Poor, which has its main entrance on Garstang Road. This home for the elderly, built round Springfield House from 1882, is still maintained by the Little Sisters of the Poor order of nuns and is named after their French founder. The part visible is the 1893 extension. In the foreground are the playing fields of Corpus Christi Catholic Sports College.

Catholic Poor Law School.

LARK HILL HOUSE SCHOOL

LARK HILL HOUSE School, Preston, 1903, drawn
by Edwin Beattie. After his brother's death,
Samuel Horrocks took over the textile empire
and needed a house which befitted his great
wealth and station. The bow-fronted section
of the convent school buildings constitutes the
original mansion built during 1796-7, and
named Lark Hill House. South facing and looking
over grassland, a lake and a screen of trees, it
was much admired and featured in architectural
publications over the 1820-50 period. Life seems
to have been eventful here: a mob attacked Lark

Hill in 1812, Samuel Horrocks Senior received a death threat and an attempt on his life, and, in contrast, there were many balls and social gatherings.

AFTER THE AMALGAMATION of the three Catholic grammar schools in 1976 following the decision to follow comprehensive education in Preston, Cardinal Newman College was established at Lark Hill in 1982. The schools which disappeared were Winckley Square Convent School and Lark Hill House School, both educating girls, and the Catholic College in Chapel Street and Winckley Square, which educated boys. The new extensions and buildings at the college have been tastefully completed and have not been constructed at the expense of established areas or, thankfully, Samuel Horrocks's residence, whose graceful late Georgian house is still at the heart of Lark Hill.

LARK HILL – THE AVENUE

LARK HILL, THE Avenue, 1908. Samuel Horrocks died in 1842 aged seventy-six, followed by his son four years later, aged forty-nine. From then on the house was not regularly lived in and was sold in 1860 for £4,525 to St Augustine's parish, assisted by wealthy Catholic merchants. A school was

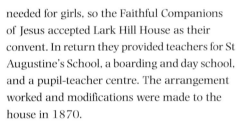

needed for girls, so the Faithful Companions of Jesus accepted Lark Hill House as their convent. In return they provided teachers for St Augustine's School, a boarding and day school, and a pupil-teacher centre. The arrangement worked and modifications were made to the house in 1870.

THIS VIEW ACROSS the terrace at Lark Hill shows the extension to the original school, built in 1908, which was completed in time for the publication of the pictorial prospectuses from which these older images come. Recently a new entry was made complete with steps. The nearest building was added in 1932 and completely blocks out the chapel extension, added in 1897, which is in full view in the 1908 photograph. As a result, the statue, fully visible in the older photograph, disappeared from view and could only be seen, as late as 1982, from a small rear window.

LARK HILL – THE HOUSE

LARK HILL, THE house and chapel, 1908. In August 1893, work began on the block to the left to provide two new classrooms and a music area with practice cubicles. On the second floor there was a chapel (damaged by fire in 1972) and a dormitory. The original portico and west entrance to the house were rebuilt facing south. In 1900 the whole building was converted to electricity and a building fund was set up in 1907. A three-day mammoth fancy fair raised enough money for work to start on improvements and extensions that same year.

THE ADDITION OF the external staircase into the east wing and its new landscaping prevented the modern photograph from being taken from the same position. In the foreground is the window of Horrocks's family parlour, from where the family could view the meadow, the lake and the

trees, which give a screen of luxuriant foliage in summer and an array of colour in autumn. Ironically, the family moved away before this effect reached maturity.

The front door and its portico were carefully moved from its original west-facing position to face south before the 1908 extension was started.

LARK HILL – THE STUDY HALL/LIBRARY

LARK HILL, THE Seniors' Study Hall, 1908. This now forms part of Cardinal Newman College Library. The school was accepted as a Direct Grant School in 1919 after satisfying certain

conditions, e.g. building a science laboratory. The greatest addition was made in 1932 and is the large three-storeyed building, including the hall, which visitors see first on entering the gate. The school went from strength to strength with rising pupil numbers after the last war. After 1967, Lark Hill took students from the Catholic high schools and did not admit junior pupils after 1977. Since 1986, Lark Hill has been the home of Cardinal Newman College, into which the sixth form was absorbed.

THIS ROOM STARTED as a study hall and later acquired a library. Currently it is the students' lounge. This view shows the modernising process the establishment has gone through. The college now offers a wide range of courses including all the sciences, performing arts, languages, law accounting, other humanities and media studies to A and AS level. The college also offers vocational BTEC courses and courses for special-needs students, along with enrichment programmes. A wide range of sports are offered, and the students perform well in sport here and academically on a national level.

Nos 23, 24 and 25 Winckley Square

WINCKLEY SQUARE CONVENT School at 23, 24 and 25 Winckley Square, 1938. In 1868 the Taunton Commission found that girls' education was severely lacking in many areas: too

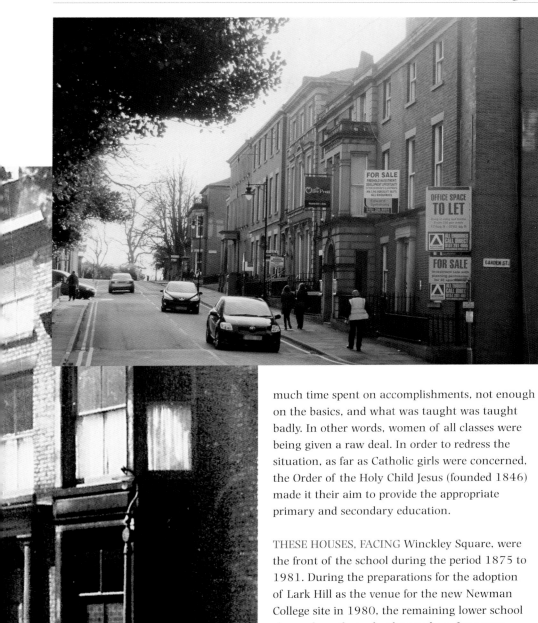

much time spent on accomplishments, not enough on the basics, and what was taught was taught badly. In other words, women of all classes were being given a raw deal. In order to redress the situation, as far as Catholic girls were concerned, the Order of the Holy Child Jesus (founded 1846) made it their aim to provide the appropriate primary and secondary education.

THESE HOUSES, FACING Winckley Square, were the front of the school during the period 1875 to 1981. During the preparations for the adoption of Lark Hill as the venue for the new Newman College site in 1980, the remaining lower school classes from that school came here for a year. In 1981 this site was closed and all the pupils, including those from this school, went to Lark Hill to finish their education. The building closest to the camera, demolished in 1958 to accommodate more classrooms, had a doorway restored in 1983, during reorganisation of the properties.

FISHERGATE, NEAR WINCKLEY STREET

HANSOM CABS IN Fishergate in 1902 by Arthur Winter. During the period between 1885 and 1914, about a dozen firms ran hire transport in the form of landaus and hansom cabs from ranks situated round the town, the largest being outside the Harris Museum. The origin of horse-drawn transport began with Richard Veevers' horse-buses in 1859; other branches

and routes were opened up to Ashton, Higher Walton and Walmer Bridge. The horse-tram operation began in 1879 with a route to Fulwood, with eight tramcars running from Guild Week 1882.

THIS STREET WITH an ancient name, the word 'gate' being the Viking name for street, continues to be a busy, commercial centre, though the flow of traffic has been east-west only since the 1960s. The bank on the corner of Lune Street occupies the site of the main druggist shop in Preston, Haverthwaite and Edmondson, where Robert Pateson worked as a shop boy. From this point he watched one of the most violent events in the city's history when a riot took place on 13 August 1842. Five cotton workers were killed during the riot and three wounded by local militia at the bottom of Lune Street.

GARSTANG ROAD, NEAR ST THOMAS'S ROAD

HORSE-DRAWN TRAM, Moor Park, near St Thomas's Road, 1903. The leases for the horse-tram system were allowed to run out on 31 December 1903 to introduce an electric system. As a consequence, places like Ashton, Farringdon Park, Fylde Road, Fulwood, Garstang Road and North Road ended up with no public transport when the 8-mile operation came to an end. Tin cans were tied to the last horse-drawn tram as it trundled home on that evening.

GARSTANG ROAD. THIS pairing shows perhaps one of the most startling 'then and now' contrasts in the whole book. The only feature of the 1903 image which survives is the gateposts on the left, and one of them has been removed in the meantime. The old photograph shows a luxuriant, sylvan suburb of the Edwardian town. The modern one shows the main A6, a dual carriageway, with traffic racing in and out of the city. St Thomas's Road corner is now open to view, as is the church of the English Martyrs. In the distance are university buildings, which stand where Moor Lane flats once did between 1962 and 2005.

FISHERGATE, NEAR GUILDHALL STREET

HORSE-DRAWN OMNIBUS, Fishergate, spring 1904. There was an immediate outcry for two reasons: fifty men had been thrown out of work and there was no public transport. This was made worse because the commencement of the electric operation was delayed from March to June 1904. As a result, horse-buses, which still worked out-of-town routes, were put back on

PRESTON FISHERGATE

Preston streets for those four months. The routes worked were limited to Fulwood, the Cemetery and Ashton. Oddly enough, no service was run to Broadgate or Farringdon Park.

THIS, PERHAPS OF all the modern images in this collection, shows the changing nature of shopping and commerce in present-day cities, with hardly a locally owned shop to be seen. On the left of the old photograph there were businesses like boot makers, confectioners, tailors and a café. On the right, where HMV are now, there was a national business, Boots the Chemists. However, the largest clothes shop was that of Alderman Frederick Matthews, whose shop was situated under the lamps on the right, where BHS stands now. He was a tireless promoter for Preston's war memorial during the years 1917-25.

CHURCH STREET
LOOKING EAST

TRAM No. 8 in Church Street, 1912. Although this tram looks like it is speeding down Church Street, it is a photographic illusion. From 1906 the maximum speed allowed for trams was 14mph, and that only on Deepdale Road. The next highest was 12mph on the double tracks on Garstang Road: the speed allowed on Church Street was 8mph. In 1925, the limit was raised to 20mph; once the fastest vehicle on the road, the tram was now only just keeping up.

THIS MODERN VIEW is one of a street that has lost its character and importance. On the extreme left of the older image is Gooby's millinery and drapery shop, which was gutted by fire in May 1965. Nearly forty years earlier, on Christmas Eve 1926, one of the shop's plate glass windows was smashed when a steam-driven lorry exploded, blowing an external fly wheel across the pavement, where the Brown family of Fletcher Road were walking by. They were all injured, but their fourteen-year-old daughter, Alice, was killed outright by the impact. She is buried in Preston Cemetery.

FRIARGATE FROM MARKET STREET

LEYLAND TITAN BUS, Friargate, 1933. By 1930 it had become obvious that buses were more suited to the newly motorised conditions in the town and the tram system would need re-planning, but nothing was done. In 1922, after many years without public transport, bus routes operated down Brook Street and Plungington Road. Trams were exchanged for buses

on the Ribbleton, Ashton, Broadgate and Farringdon Park routes.

ST WALBURGE'S SPIRE, the tallest of any parish church in Britain, is probably the oldest feature of both photographs. This end of Friargate was widened and refashioned in 1893, destroying many courts, ginnels, shops and eating houses to accommodate Market Street, which runs to the right. The building on the corner, which for many years housed a bank, is now the premises of a turf accountant. Benjamin Franklin lived for a short time in the town and his blue plaque is on the wall of the second white building on the right, which stands on the corner of Orchard Street.

JUNCTION OF WATERY LANE, STRAND ROAD AND WATER LANE

WATERY LANE, STRAND Road and Water Lane Junction, 1910. In the centre, facing each other, are the Grand Junction at No. 7 Watery Lane (built 1855) and the Wheatsheaf at No. 50 Water Lane (built 1857), which lost its name as part of a gimmick in 1994. Its proximity to the dock made it a centre for maritime businesses such as timber merchants, china clay merchants, ship-owners, chandlers, ship-stores

and all kinds of dock management. The photograph was probably taken on a Sunday and gives a false impression of peacefulness.

THE LAMP ON the older image says 'Danger', which could have been a warning to the author when taking the modern photograph, as this area is always busy with traffic, despite the impression the photograph may give. The shuttering and barriers on the left hide the tunnels and shafts being dug to work on the quality of water in the Ribble Estuary and on the Fylde coast. The Grand Junction still prospers and the Wheatsheaf across from it has had its original name rightfully restored recently. Notice how much this end of Strand Road has been widened over the years.

PARK ROAD/ RINGWAY FROM NORTH ROAD

THE JUNCTION OF North Road with Meadow Street and Park Road, *c.*1955. The car on the left, just visible, is entering Meadow Street, while the road stretching away is Park Road. Two of the spirelets on St Paul's church can just be glimpsed through the chimneys. North Road and its junction with Walker Street would be to the right. All this was demolished in 1964 to make way for Ringway, the dual carriageway ring road to the north of the town centre. Of all the buildings in Park Road, only the former St Paul's church survives. In February 1965, the *Lancashire Evening Post* reported many large piles of bricks, described as eyesores, lying around in

Walker Street, Lancaster Road and North Road, encouraging petty lawbreaking in premises still standing and hindering police work. In June 1967 Cyril Heywood of the *Post* commented, 'As we look disconsolately on the rubble strewn on the demolition sites on which the Preston of the future is taking shape, we should take heart that we are not the only Prestonians who have seen their town laid to waste to make way for what optimists always feel will be better days to come.' Many Prestonians feel they never came.

THE ONLY REFERENCE point in this incongruous pairing is the spirelets of St Paul's church on the left side of both photographs. It has been some time since the building was a church, having closed its doors for the last time in 1973. Samuel Horrocks of Lark Hill fame is buried in the churchyard. Red Rose Radio took over the empty building in 1981 and has broadcast as Rock FM since 1990. Park Road has ceased to exist as Ringway, that ring road which runs *through* the city, races away towards the junction with Church Street.

GARSTANG ROAD FROM AQUEDUCT STREET

CORNER OF GARSTANG Road and Aqueduct Street, August 1953. Aqueduct Street is in the foreground: note the absence of traffic lights. On the left is Garstang Road, running further on into Moor Lane. Round the corner from the hoardings is the Albert Billiard Hall. Further along, past the Garstang Road hoardings, was Mather's Printers, whose premises were finally demolished in September 1995. On the hoardings, the top row advertise fairly commonplace items, but the others are more local and advertise events commencing on 7 September 1953. The Empire cinema

was about to show an 'adults only' feature for that week. The Empire started as a revue theatre in 1911, showing occasional films, and was a permanent cinema from 1930 to 1964 when it became a bingo hall. It was demolished in 1974. The Palace, advertising a revue, was built on the site of an old skating rink in Tithebarn Street and opened in 1913 as a theatre, though it did show films at times. It was closed in 1955, and lay empty and derelict before being demolished to make way for the new bus station in 1967. The Royal Hippodrome is advertising another play by the Salberg Players during their successful eight-year residence there. The Harris Institute is putting forward its new year of educational courses and the Royal Liverpool Philharmonic Orchestra were about to make one of its regular visits to the Public Hall.

ONLY ONE OF the five trees remains, but not much else. On the right is a DIY store which has taken up the area once occupied by some houses in Aqueduct Street, a snooker club, Cartmell and Barlow's coffin works and the premises of Mather's Printers. This firm were printers for five generations in Preston, from 1859 to 1986. Moor Lane runs to the right, in the distance, and North Road to the left. Between the demolition of hundreds of houses during 1962-4 along these roads, and the maisonettes and university residences being built in this decade, blocks of flats on Moor Lane were built and demolished.

Other titles published by The History Press

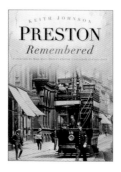

Preston Remembered
KEITH JOHNSON

A fascinating collection of articles written by author and *Lancashire Evening Post* historian Keith Johnson. Take a nostalgic journey into Preston's colourful past, recalling the events that transformed this historic cotton town into a university city. Take a peep at the days of cotton mills, factories, public houses and endless rows of terraced homes that shaped the lives of many. Richly illustrated with over 50 images, this nostalgic volume will appeal to everyone who knows this part of Lancashire.

978 0 7524 6035 2

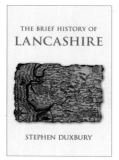

The Brief History of Lancashire
STEPHEN DUXBURY

The Brief history of Lancashire starts with the beginning – the moment when the detritus of a dying star, spinning through the depths of the Milky Way, began to cool and coalesce, and rain (typically for Lancashire) began to fall as the moisture in the new atmosphere began to condense. A planet was formed, and history as we know it began. Racing through the history of Lancashire, this book will tell you everything you should know about the dramatic and fascinating history of the county, and a few things you never thought you would.

978 0 7524 6288 2

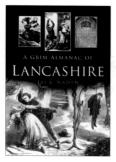

A Grim Almanac of Lancashire
JACK NADIN

A Grim Almanac of Lancashire is a day-by-day catalogue of 365 ghastly tales from around the county dating from the twelfth to the twentieth centuries. Full of dreadful deeds, macabre deaths, strange occurrences and heinous homicides, this almanac explores the darker side of the county's past. If you have ever wondered about what nasty goings-on occurred in the Lancashire of yesteryear, then look no further. But do you have the stomach for it?

978 0 7524 5684 3

Infamous Lancashire Women
ISSY SHANNON

From the notorious Pendle Witches, whose nefarious activities in the seventeenth century led to death and disaster, to the reviled Myra Hindley, the most hated woman in modern criminal history, Issy Shannon's new book is a riveting roll-call of Lancashire women truly deserving of the title 'infamous'. Alongside the Manchester baby-farmer and the unfortunate Lady Mabel Bradshaw of Wigan, who unwittingly committed bigamy, are witches, fraudsters, cross-dressers and thieves and women notorious as mistresses to the highest in the land.

978 0 7509 4969 9

Visit our website and discover thousands of other History Press books.

www.thehistorypress.co.uk